All Scripture references taken from the KJV of the Holy Bible, unless otherwise indicated.

Here Come the Horns
by Dr. Marlene Miles
Freshwater Press 2025
freshwaterpress9@gmail.com

ISBN: 978-1-965772-92-8

eBook Version

Table of Contents

Four Horns and Four Craftsmen...................4

Warning...................6

What Horns?...................12

Horns: Instruments of Sound...................17

Animal Horns...................19

Divine Horns of God...................25

The Devil has Horns, So They Say...................30

Horny; That Little *Horn*...................33

Demonic Fighting Horns...................44

Bulls of Bashan...................46

Bully...................54

Signs that Spiritual Horns are Warring Against You...................58

Blow the Trumpet in Zion...................63

How to Fight the Horns...................64

Divine Carpenters...................68

Men Skilled to Destroy...................73

The Lifter of My Head...................76

Under Judgment?...................97

Psalm 54:1-7...................103

Divine Axe of the Lord...................105

Divine Scroll of God...................107

Warfare Section 118

Dear Reader 124

Appendix 125

Prayerbooks by this author 126

Other books by this author 128

Four Horns and Four Craftsmen

Then I looked up, and there before me were four horns.

I asked the angel who was speaking to me, "What are these?"

He answered me, "These are the horns that scattered Judah, Israel and Jerusalem."

Then the Lord showed me four craftsmen.

I asked, "What are these coming to do?"

He answered, "These are the horns that scattered Judah so that no one could raise their head, but the craftsmen have come to terrify them and throw down these horns of the nations who lifted up their horns against the land of Judah to scatter its people."   (Zechariah 1:18-21)

Here Come the Horns

Freshwater

Warning

Saints of God, we are going to start this book out very simply and then we will go deep.

Let me warn you about something I learned the hard way. what a man says is highly significant. What a man prays is even more significant. We all know that, so I want to share something that happened to me because I assisted the enemy in sending me something that I didn't want, by <u>singing</u> it in a secular song. For decades, and even up until now I've been very careful of choosing my *spoken* words so they wouldn't be used against me. But there I was just humming and singing away, mindlessly.

Oh, it doesn't matter what you sing, it's just music, you may argue.

It matters, folks. If you've never gotten what you said---, especially something bad, then thank God. If it has never happened to you, then pray now and cancel all negative or evil words that you have spoken, vowed, sworn to, sang, agreed with – all your words. If you even think that you have spoken from your mouth something that you now regret having said and you definitely don't want the words you spoke to happen to you, your life or your loved ones, renounce those words now. Do it now and try to stop it from happening and hopefully you still have time.

`` Singing is praying. Praying is saying a thing at least once, praying to God or some higher power. But repeating a thing over and again is still praying and it is meditation, and it can be very powerful.

A man can have what he says.

Many would argue that this is not true. Well, my Bible says that, so it is true. Even though you may not mean it as prayer, the fact that it is your meditation, with or without music, drums, or any type of rhythm or syncopation, it is still prayer. Saying it over and over is meditation.

Music addiction? What is that? I know more than one person who cannot stand quiet. There must be noise, specifically music playing in their car, in their work environment, in their home, In their ears all the time. Some people can't sleep without noise, ambient sounds, or TV, or music, at full blast. Some of those people have told me that my house is too quiet.

Personally, I may keep the Bible playing, or worship music or prayers while I sleep, but very, very quiet so it is heard in the spirit but not in my sleeping ears. I suppose some can't stand their own thoughts or whatever *voices* are in their heads, so they try to drown those voices with more *voices*. Music.

The devil is not just planning that we will love music, he plans to get us addicted to it and then later use it as a weapon. He uses music to distract us, to stop us from praying or reading the Bible, or just sitting still and listening to God. He uses music, specifically to get us to say things that we would never normally say and to repeat, that is *pray* things that we would never consider as prayer or consider praying. Not only that, while we are involved with our devices that blast sounds, voices, and music, our entire being is involved if we are mentally focused on what we hear, and especially if our bodies dance, sway, jump, leap, wave,---, *boogie*--, whatever we do when we are enthralled in song or music.

It is the words of these songs that the devil wants us to say, sing, and repeat that can cause so much harm. These words are not only **not** devil proofed, but they are also designed to be God proofed, peace proofed, success proofed. These words open the doors to our life for the enemy to step right in. These words are the opposite of what is in the Bible, out of the mouth of God, or in the meditation of your own heart or should never be words of your own mouth.

I don't need to give you a list of examples, just apply the Word of God to any words you hear as "music" and any words that you sing, especially if you have been singing those words for many years, because it's your *jam*.

Words, especially in English can have so many meanings. How you say a thing and what you mean is what you mean, but if that same word can be used by the devil against you, or misused against you, your spouse, children, family, health, business, destiny helpers, anyone you pray with or for, then that is what he will do.

You don't know what you don't know.

I did not know what I did not know. Many years ago, I liked a song called, **Here Come the Horns**. I didn't live in the culture of that band or people who listened or partied to that song. I didn't even know what culture listened to that music, I stumbled on the song one day when asking Alexa for an entirely different song. I listened and thought the song was funny and kind of cute. I also know that my body liked the beat and the singer's voice, and I liked the sound of the horns. When that song was played, I would automatically boogie, which is no reason to choose a song.

In that song, I didn't know what *horns* were, or what they were singing about. The album cover showed silhouettes of a mariachi style band, so who knew? Before seeing the cover art, I imagined it was about low-rider cars, so maybe it was about car horns?

After seeing the cover, I thought the song was about musical instruments or the section of the band that played those instruments. Yes, it was. And it was about anything else called a horn, especially anything the devil could use against me as I sang that song so many times, even in the privacy of my own home while cleaning, or in my own kitchen while cooking. So, singing those lyrics meant that I was announcing a band playing wind instruments? Hmmm.

What Horns?

What does the Word of God say that horns are?

The *four horns of the Altar* refer to the four projections at the corners of Old Testament altars. These horns were involved in the religious ceremonies and practices of ancient Israel.

An altar in those days was an active thing. There were different types of sacrifices, but the animal sacrifices were brought to the priest alive, and in good condition. The animals were tied to the horns of the altar, else, they'd be running all over the place.

God is the LORD, which hath shewed us light: bind the sacrifice with cords, even unto the horns of the altar. (Psalm 118:27)

Nowadays, this concept may be difficult to grasp because we don't bring animals to church. Furthermore, these days, many churches don't even have an altar and those that do simply have a table where they put communion bread and wine, if that church even does communion. The place in front and center of the church where the pastor stands is called the altar, but there is nothing physical there to represent an Old Testament altar which was a physical structure, in plain sight, in Bible days.

Since Jesus was the ultimate sacrifice, some may argue that sacrifices are no longer necessary, but that is the subject for another book, another day.

Many "churches" these days are set up as theatres where shows are put on. But stay with us as we continue to discuss this.

An altar doesn't have to be physical; it can be a spiritual and therefore invisible altar. So, we can describe an altar as a place and as a designation of what goes on in a place with regularity with the purpose of connecting the natural world to the spiritual world. The purpose is to connect man with God. There can be evil altars, however, where man attempts to connect with whatever deity he is serving that is NOT Jehovah God; that is how it is designated as an evil altar.

We serve Jehovah God. Only. And, Amen.

God graciously told man how to make the altar that would work for Him.

"Make a horn at each of the four corners, so that the horns and the altar are of one piece, and overlay the altar with bronze." (Exodus 27:2)

These physical horn extensions were used in several ways. Sacrificial blood was applied to the horns for atonement. According to Scripture:

In the sin offering, the priest would "put some of the blood on the horns of the altar of fragrant incense before the LORD." (Leviticus 4:7)

People seeking sanctuary from retribution could grasp the horns of the altar as a plea for mercy. Adonijah, fearing for his life, "went and took hold of the horns of the altar." (1 Kings 1:50).

Unfortunately, there are churches by nefarious political activities that seem to have lost their sanctuary status as of the writing of this book. Not only that, but the church is also desecrated by, greed, lust, fake pastors, fake prophets, Freemasons, witches, the occult, sin and even robbers, gunmen and active shooters in this country and all over the world.

Horns, in Scripture, also represent the power and strength of God. They represent God's' covenant with Israel and remind us of the divine authority and protection that the altar signifies.

However, people with their demons on board are not afraid of God, consequences and have no respect for the House of God, as they should.

Four horns on that altar symbolize all points of the Earth, north, south, east and west--, God has got it covered. God can forgive, provide for us and make atonement through His great Mercy toward us, no matter where we are.

Other religions also had altars, and their altars also had horns, but God gave specific instructions to Israel for the construction and use of the altar and its *horns*. So, these horns were to the benefit of mankind; these *horns* were of God, and for His purposes and to benefit mankind; they were good.

Horns: Instruments of Sound

Nowadays and in the most common usage, we think of horns as trumpets and trombones and shofars. Since synthesizers became the rage last century, we don't see a horn section in bands like we used to, but there are still fine musicians who study and play those instruments very well. We see and hear horn sections in symphonies and orchestras. Modern horns as musical instruments, as said, are the wind instruments and I'm sure you can name a couple or a few.

As said, when I sang those words, *here come the horns*, I really thought I was singing about musical instruments. But the devil could take those unframed words and frame them to his specifications and if I was ever in his crosshairs, he may have been able to use that against me. As you read on you will find out that I'm pretty sure he did.

That's what we may mean when we say such a thing, but what can be implied based on our own words? The variety in horn history includes fingerhole horns, the natural horn, Russian horns, French horn, Vienna horn, mellophone, saxhorn (saxophone), marching horn, and Wagner tuba.

Michael Segell wrote a book entitled, *The Devil's Horn* where he expounds on the history of the saxophone. Beginning with "a sound never heard before," Segell follows the instrument as it is lauded for its sensuality, then outlawed for its influence, and finally credited with changing the face of popular culture. That doesn't mean that the saxophone or any other instrument is demonic. God created music and musical instruments. It is how they are used that makes them good or evil.

Here come the horns? I am not an emcee, and it is not my job to introduce the band or any portion of it.

So, now, as I should have back then, ask myself, why sing that song?

Animal Horns

Why sing the words, *here come the horns*, or any other lyrics to any other secular song? None of that praises God. Surely, I wasn't announcing animal horns, car horns, the symphony, or any other kind of horn.

What's the difference between horns and antlers, anyway?

On animals, horns are permanent; antlers are not. **Horns** are projections from the top of the head. True horns are found mainly among cattle, goats, antelopes and pronghorns. This is a list of animals that have hard permanent pointed projections on their head.

Of note, the shofar, which is a horn made from the horn of a sheep or ram is blown as a call to prayer or worship in Israel. It is the only horn made from a horn and used as an instrument called a horn would normally be used--, to make a sound.

Horned animals are the addax, bull, cows, goats, rams, ibex, oryx, markhor, kudu, buffalo, bighorn sheep, wildebeest, springbok, gazelle, yak, and others.

- Giraffes have *ossicones* that they use in necking contests to fight other giraffes.

- Most deer, mule deer, elk, caribou, and moose have antlers, which are not true horns due to lacking a bone core.

- Rhinoceros "horns" are made of keratin but there is no bone within them.

- For fun, I add that a unicorn's horn is a horn and not an antler because it doesn't deciduate, that is it stays on. Unicorns are mentioned six different times, in six different places in the Bible, so they are not make-believe. *Are they?* If they are real, I'm sure they are not rainbow colored.

But my horn shalt thou exalt like *the horn of* an **unicorn**: I shall be anointed with fresh oil. (Psalm 92:10)

Tusks are teeth; they are not horns at all. They are found on elephants, walruses, and warthogs.

Animals use their horns to defend themselves and also to exert dominance, to mark, claim and maintain territory. During mating season, horn fighting is done within members of the species and group for territory, dominance or mating priority. Outside of attack and defense, animals may use horns to dig for food in the soil or peel bark off trees. They may also feature in mating displays, and the blood vessels inside horns help to maintain the animal's body temperature.

Horns are usually present only in males but in some species, females may have horns. These horns that scattered Judah, Israel and Jerusalem were spiritual.

1. Lord, let any horns coming up against me, my life, my destiny or any one I pray for or anyone I have stewardship over begin to fight for dominance and territory amongst themselves, to their own demise, in the Name of Jesus.

The word "bullhorn" is believed to originate from the combination of "bull" and "horn," likely referencing the shape of a bull's horn which is similar to the cone-shaped design of a device used to amplify sound, suggesting a connection to the idea of using a loud voice to control a crowd. The use of a loud voice can control a herd or a large group of animals, or people. A rancher might use a loud voice to round up his cattle. The exact origin of the term is not known. But somehow a rancher seems to know that if you tell your cattle what to do, they will do it.

Jacob, who was ranching on Laban's farm, by divine Wisdom seemed to know that if you show your cattle what to do, they will do it. This proves that a man can have what he says, what he prays and that we have dominion over the animals which are the works of God's hands.

And Jacob did separate the lambs, and set the faces of the flocks toward the ringstraked, and all the brown in the flock of Laban; and he put his own flocks by themselves, and put them not unto Laban's cattle. (Genesis 30:40)

And the man increased exceedingly, and had much cattle, and maidservants, and menservants, and camels, and asses. (Genesis 30:43)

That's the four-legged world with all those horns and thank God they are mostly herbivores. There are many species of beetles and caterpillars that also have horns. Also, the Jackson chameleon has horns. They are small so we don't worry too much about them. However, that is a problem with man; just because it is small doesn't mean that we shouldn't pay attention to it. Even if something is invisible, as many spiritual things are, doesn't mean we should ignore it, either. Still, we thank God that there are no horned, carnivorous animals that are predators to man. This doesn't mean that large horned animals won't fight, but man is not in their food chain, although they may be in man's diet. It doesn't mean that if provoked that they won't fight and defend themselves from others of their own species and against man. This is why man attempts to train these large animals to work for him. It is the wild, or provoked horned animals that have been attempted to be domesticated, that can represent the most danger.

Yes, I'm saying that it is the animal that you've brought to your own farm, ranch, or compound that can attack if it feels threatened or if it is provoked.

Just to bookend this, the human bully does not feel provoked, he is the provocateur. The spiritual horn, whether it is provoked or not, if it sees an opening it will attack a person's life, livelihood, marriage, family, business, ministry, and destiny. It is a bully in that it comes with a demonic power and if a person is not paying attention, they may just be walking around as a regular human, not "powered up" in prayer to fight the horns, whether they are announced or not.

In my case, I was singing about something that may have come to try to beset me but still didn't know that it was coming as an attack or what to do about it. Please read on so you can stop this from happening to you. But if it does, learn to be prayed up so you won't be caught flatfooted if evil *horns* come up against you.

Divine Horns of God

For every beast of the forest is mine, and the cattle upon a thousand hills. (Psalms 50:10)

The word, *horn* appears throughout both the Old and New Testaments. It describes strength, power, authority, and divine intervention. In the above verse in Psalms, it represents wealth and prosperity; cattle in that time period was their currency. God is rich in silver and gold and owns all the cattle. If a man had cattle, he was wealthy, or even very wealthy. In our times, we think of millionaires and billionaires as wealthy. In Bible days if you were a *cattle-aire*, or a *cattle-heir,* you were very rich.

So the LORD blessed the latter end of Job more than his beginning: for he had fourteen thousand sheep, and six thousand camels, and a thousand yoke of oxen, and a thousand she asses (Job 42:12)

The horn's symbolism is rooted in the contexts of their day and linked to the might and majesty of animals such as oxen and rams. If you had animals such as that; you had a work force. You had food. You could use the hides for clothing. You had trading power, and you also had a way to serve, worship and sacrifice to God. Basically, you had everything.

In the Bible, the horn, therefore, symbolizes strength and power, particularly military might and victory.

His majesty is like a firstborn bull, and his horns are like the horns of a wild ox. With them he will gore the nations, even those at the ends of the earth.(Deuteronomy 33:17)

In this Scripture, *horn* represents the power and dominance that Joseph's descendants will wield over their enemies.

Hannah's prayer makes reference to the horn as a symbol of strength.

Those who oppose the LORD will be shattered; He will thunder from heaven against them. The LORD will judge the ends of the earth. He will give strength to His king and exalt the horn of His anointed. (2 Samuel 2:10)

The exaltation of the horn of a nation, a people, or even an individual person, such as a king, signifies the empowerment and victory of God's chosen.

The horn is also a symbol of authority and kingship.

"The ten horns are ten kings who will rise from this kingdom. After them another king, different from the earlier ones, will rise and subdue three kings." (Daniel 7:24)

In the Book of Revelation horns represent political and spiritual powers. Ten horns represent ten kings who have not yet received a kingdom, but will receive authority for a short time. But note here that these ten kings will receive power "with the beast" so they are not anointed by God who anoints kings and nations with divine authority and power. The devil is a copycat, so he plans to do the same at the appointed evil time:

"The ten horns you saw are ten kings who have not yet received a kingdom, but will receive authority as kings with the beast for one hour." (Revelation 17:12)

In many movies depicting ancient kingdoms, the trumpets herald the entrance of the king, especially if he is returning victoriously from battle. In this country the president's song is *Hail to the Chief* and it is laden with horns, trumpets and other regal instruments.

The horn is also a symbol of divine intervention and salvation.

The LORD is my rock, my fortress, and my deliverer. My God is my rock, in whom I take refuge, my shield, and the horn of my salvation, my stronghold." (Psalm 18:2)

Here, the horn of salvation signifies God's power to save and deliver His people from their adversaries.

New Testament, Zechariah, the father of John the Baptist, prophesies about the coming of the Messiah, referring to Him as a "horn of salvation." This speaks of Messiah's role as Deliverer and Savior.

"He has raised up a horn of salvation for us in the house of His servant David" (Luke 1:69)

The horn is associated with anointing and consecration. In ancient Israel, the horn of an animal was often used as a vessel for holding anointing oil such as that poured by

Samuel when he anointed David as king. Anointing empowers a person for service.

"So Samuel took the horn of oil and anointed him in the presence of his brothers, and the Spirit of the LORD rushed upon David from that day forward." (1 Samuel 16:13)

Horn is authority and power. It represents the transference of the same, as well.

As you can see, one word can mean, depict, and represent a lot of things. So, we can now see how if a word is used in some random or freestanding way that it can be captured, as it were, and twisted and misused by anyone or anything who wants to do that. Therefore, we must **devil proof** our words and not let our lips be loose enough to sink any ship.

Zechariah's vision speaks of the horns that scattered, Judah, Israel and Jerusalem... Horns that scatter. Does your life seem scattered? Do your efforts seem scattered? How about your marriage, or your children?

There could be spiritual horns working against you. What are some of the signs of Evil Horns working against you?

The Devil has Horns, So They Say

The devil has horns? Yeah, that's what they say. It's those pointy things coming out of his head is how he is pictured in many images. Lucifer was created by God, and I can't say that God put horns on him, but as he fell from Heaven and his name was changed to Satan, perhaps as his nature and purpose and goals changed, so did his appearance. Horns are made to scatter, maim, intimidate, bully, hurt, and kill. The devil has taken that as his self-assigned evil against mankind, so perhaps he does now have horns.

In the Bible, the term "horn" is a metaphor for a nation's strength, power, and authority. It can also symbolize a nation's military might. The devil has power. He is not more powerful than God, and without God we cannot oppose that level of evil, so don't play.

Examples of horns in the Bible:

- **Four horns:** in the Book of Zechariah, four horns represent the four nations that scattered Israel.

- **Little horn:** in Daniel 7:8, a little horn grows from the midst of ten horns on a beast that represents a kingdom. The little horn speaks against God and oppresses his people.

- **Raised horn:** in Psalm 148, the psalmist calls for all creatures to praise God, with the raised horn symbolizing victory.

Prayer point:

2. Raise my horn, O Lord, in the Name of Jesus.

- **Horn of salvation:** Zacharias prophesied Jesus' deliverance for mankind.

In Christian drawings, horns on the head of a person or supernatural being are usually signs of evil. Depending on the purpose of doing it, a person might buy costume prosthetic horns for their evil holidays or other events. Either people do this because they think it is funny, or they are serious Satan worshippers.

- God destroys His enemies, spoken of as the evil horns; He does this by His Divine Craftsman and other divine weapons.

The evil *horns* represented the Gentile nations that scattered God's covenant people into exile. The horn metaphor appears multiple times in the Scriptures, most notably in prophetic visions, where the horns symbolize nations or kingdoms that rise up against God's people. In the Book of Zechariah, for example, a vision reveals four horns representing the nations that have scattered Israel.

So, we can surmise that the devil has horns. He has empowered groups, nations, or even individuals to do harm to others, specifically to do harm to God's people. Those horns act in various ways, and some of those ways are subtle. The devil's deception is so deep that at least one of those ways can be pleasurable---, *at first.*

Horny; That Little *Horn*

Horny, by definition means, of or resembling a horn. It can also mean feelings of being aroused or sexually excited. Synonyms include: feeling sexy, sexually aroused, excited, stimulated, amorous, lustful, turned on, or on fire.

Just because you can't stop fantasizing about a person, does not mean that that thought is your own thought; it could have been sent to you. Do not think that just because you are thinking about a person, either innocently or sexually means that they are also thinking of you in the same way, or at all. That is a lie that you should not believe. How many of you have ever gotten a "friend suggestion" on social media, and then clicked on it because you thought the person was asking you to friend them, only to find out that the computer sent that "friend request" and the other person knows nothing about the "request"? But, while you're at it, as long as you've clicked on them, now the algorithm goes to that person and says that **you** are now requesting to be friends with them on this social media platform.

The devil works like that, too. He could have sent amorous thoughts to just you, or to two of you and whoever responds first is the biggest sucker. Whoever responds first may be the weakest, spiritually speaking. Now that you are properly deceived, you are on the phone trying to make a date with this object of your desire who may not have even given a thought about you.

Demonic *horns* are a thing, and we will dig deeper to find out what they are about and what we can do about them. The devil uses that little horn that men have, to oppress and make war with God's people.

The *little horn* in Daniel 7:8, a little horn grows from the midst of ten horns on a beast that represents a kingdom. The little horn speaks against God and oppresses His people.

A little horn doesn't have to be a physical appendage, although it could be. There may be a little horn in <u>any</u> person, that part that is still in the flesh, likes revenge, wants payback, is greedy or lustful, for example. That little horn makes people into Karens. That little horn may be temporal and fall off after winter like antlers deciduate from deer. But it may be permanent, unfortunately like a real horn. That little horn, even if it is hidden, is the foothold that the devil has in anyone; it will oppress others and also make that person go astray from the plan of God.

Jesus said the devil had nothing in Him; can we say the same?

Every sexual thought you have is not necessarily your own thought--, even thoughts that make you feel horny. All sin is by invitation. The idea to sin pops into your head--, where did it come from?

Well, if it's sin, you don't need but one guess: the devil.

Signs of horniness: You're restless; this could also be a *sent* affect. You're aroused or tingling; it's that *little horn* in a man that is the receptor for this signal that the devil sends. Women have *little horns*, too.

Having feelings of arousal or feelings that you want to have *relations* still may not be your idea. If the enemy wants to entice you to sin, especially sexual sin, then why not stimulate you there?

How is this possible?

Spirit spouse. Your entire body may be under control of lustful or other *spirits* especially if you've given in to your lust over and again for years and years. Just because you feel this stimulation in your physical body doesn't mean that you are in control of it, or that the person you're thinking of is wishing they could do this that or the other to you – necessarily.

However, it is possible for you to know if someone is thinking up some funny business with you in mind; it depends on your level of discernment. But it also means that you need to pray and put a stop to that. Don't give in to it or allow it. The devil or some demon that he has sent is **in** every illegal sex act. Every one of them. Legal sex is with your legally married spouse, only. No, don't yell at a person or call them up and tell them off if you pick up in the spirit that they are up to some hanky panky with you in mind. Instead, pray. Handle this in prayer, decrees, and declarations.

How many people have you heard of who do things, even sexual things and then later cannot say how it happened, or why it happened. This does not mean that the person is lying or trying to get out of some trouble they've gotten into--, they may really be oppressed or even possessed of the devil and are under the control of the devil and or his agents. They really may not be able to control themselves, or they can't control themselves after they get to a certain point in foreplay or the sex act.   Remember, you can't fight demonic power without the power of God. Yes, it's demonic, so stay prayed up so you aren't that demonized person or end up in a sexual situation with a demonized person.

Perhaps you've been programmed to turn to sex as an escape mechanism. You may call it a high sex drive, and it may be, but is it of God? Is it Godly? Is it ruining or threatening to ruin your life, destiny, career, or relationships? That's not of God or from God. Is it higher than what should be normal for a human being, and you know it is? Then, that is lust driven. Your body is being used to try to satisfy a demon, or demons, and you may not even know it. It could be fun--, at first, but then you will get so tired of it because it is not of God. It may be entirely the opposite of your real personality or temperament. It could be that you are being driven into those temptations, sins, and transgressions. Not only that, you are the one who will have to pay for the iniquity that results from sin and transgressions, and that could be sooner rather than later, or sooner and also later. **This depends on why the devil would want you to sin sexually; it is not for the sex, there is something more behind it; there always is.**

The world invites those who feel the *urge* to give into it. The Bible says bring your body under. The world says go for it; the Bible says do not walk after the flesh. The world says go ahead and scratch that itch or masturbate to make it go away.

That will not only not make it go away, it will invite more demons. Masturbation is worship to the demons who are inciting your mind and maybe even your physical body to perform this very act. If you can't find anyone to do it with, then doing it alone or with objects is still demonic worship.

While you are in this act, the thoughts and images in your mind are indicative of *who* this worship is to. Hate to break it to you, but aside from the plastic surgery, many porn stars are not even real or whole people; they are from the evil marine kingdom. Whether you are queuing up porn on your devices, or conjuring up porn images in your mind, doing either is worshipping idols from the marine kingdom. What you worship is your "*god*."

It is no coincidence that being horny and acting ungodly because of it can cause demonic attack, oppression, possession or even worse things. We just said that the illegal sex is to accomplish another goal, such as to steal, kill, or destroy. Where in the Bible does it say that the devil's end game is to make people sin sexually? No, Balaam was sent to CURSE Israel, Balack sent in sex workers to get them to SIN so Balaam could then CURSE them.

When Balaam couldn't curse Israel, Balack got the wise idea to get them to sin so they would then be curse-able. What sin? Sexual sin, then nearly 40,000 of them were killed after they sinned with the women that were sent in to entice them to sin. Horniness may be called that for just that reason---, after any sin, but especially sexual sin, evil *horns* can be sent in to spiritually attack the unrepentant sinner.

Jacob's sons tricked the men of Shechem into getting circumcised, then on the third day they were all too weak to fight, Shechem was raided and taken. All the little "horns" of those men were hurt, having been circumcised, weakening those men, supposedly temporarily. This mass circumcision was a trick that was done because the prince of that city, Hamor's *little horn* violated Jacob's daughter Dinah, and the entire city of Shechem paid for it. One man's **horniness** and subsequent sexual sin caused the demise of an entire city. The people of a city or land are subject to what the leader allows. When Hamor assaulted Dinah it was as though he was saying, not *here's Johnny*, but *here come the horns*.

If you or me, or anyone is going to announce something like, *here come the horns*, it should be to prophesy to yourself, your family, and even the city, calling for repentance so the attack does not hurt you and those you have authority over.

On the flip side, if you do find that your spontaneous horniness is impacting your daily life or you find yourself asking "Why do I feel hornier than normal," pray. You may need to seek deliverance from a trusted deliverance minister. Don't just go to sex addicts anonymous and meet more sex addicts who are trying to get over sex addictions by using their minds only or some psychological or New Age type process. Now you're in a room full of sex addicts, all of whom have no control over their demons. What do you think will happen in that setting? Possibly more sex, unless the addicts have really learned their lessons and hit rock bottom.

3. Lord, anything, person, or power that has taken control over my libido, I break their power over my life, in the Name of Jesus.

4. Lord, return my libido back to normal, not too high, and not to low, but to the praise of Your Glory, in the Name of Jesus. Amen.

Certain foods are said to be aphrodisiacs and are known to inspire or feed into the sexual lust of people. Many drugs have been created to assist in sexual sin. You may say it is not a sin if it is with your own spouse, but that depends. The marriage bed is to be undefiled. What is your intention of doing this sex act? Is it with your lawful married spouse? Are your intentions pure with your spouse and when in the act? Then your marriage bed is undefiled. Anything other is defiling and that defilement is not just for the sake of the defilement; it is for something far worse that may be hidden to you. Better ask God.

Speaking of aphrodisiacs and pharmaceutical sexual support, an over-the-counter supplement called horny goat weed is also known as *yin yang huo*. It has limited evidence of real health benefits but might help increase blood flow to certain areas of the body to improve sexual function. I am not recommending it; I'm only telling you about it. People use it for E.D. as well as for other sexual problems, brittle bones, and post-menopausal symptoms. It is used for a number of other things too, according to WebMD, but there is not enough evidence to confirm that this supplement works for those issues.

Well, if the horns have not been successful to entice you to sin or support you in sinning or being able to continue sinning, or even if they have, now they may be used to fight you or oppress you. After all, the devil's nature is to turn on a person even if he first presented as an angel of light, or as a friend. Eventually, he will turn on a man.

Demonic Fighting Horns

Horns are an escalation of warfare against a man or mankind. If I had known that, I would have never, ever, ever sang, or casually spoken the words announcing or inviting *horns* into my life or environment. The word *horn*, itself can be used, but I should have been the most specific person ever to clearly say what *horn* I was talking about.

Horns are indicative or represent or depict power. What power?

For we wrestle not against flesh and blood, but against principalities, against **powers**, against the rulers of the darkness of this world, against spiritual wickedness in high places. (Ephesians 6:12, *emphasis mine*)

All of that wickedness in high places is powerful if not dealt with or opposed, or shall

I say, wrestled with. Horns represent *powers*. Note that it is not one singular power, but plural *powers*. This is an escalation against the intended victim and therefore the saint of God needs to be more vigilant, more prayerful, walk upright, repent, get in the Word, stay in the Word, and speak and pray the Word.

Jesus used the Word to beat the devil in His Wilderness temptations. What level of spiritual wickedness was the devil? He was the top of that food chain from Ephesians 6:12. So, be sure to use the weapons of God to fight the horns. We will go into that later in this volume as well.

Looking again at my mistake, do not ever announce the arrival of *horns*, unless you mean the Horn of the Lord, the Horn of Salvation, the horn of God's protection and power, or even the horn of plenty which we learned in school correlates to prosperity or an abundant harvest. Be specific when you use that word.

Bulls of Bashan

Horns arrive. Ancient bulls, with their horns, and they've certainly got horns---, sinister ones. If you are announcing them, it's the same as inviting them. So don't do it. You may not have done anything to allow horns into your life, but your ancestors may have allowed them into your bloodline. They may have lain dormant without a way to get in, but by announcing them... here they come!

Be not far from me; for trouble is near; for there is none to help.

Many bulls have compassed me: strong bulls of Bashan have beset me round. What or who are these "strong bulls of Bashan?"
(Psalm 22:11-12)

There are many prophetic visions in the Bible; Psalm 22 is one because David is writing about what is happening to Jesus on the Cross. In the case of Psalm 22, however, we cannot see why God's Word is about *literal* animals in that situation. Something more sinister is going on; it is spiritual.

People have gathered to watch the Son of God suffer and die, they've beaten Him, scourged Him, mocked Him, scattered His clothing by casting lots for it. If you smite the shepherd the sheep will scatter. The Cross for Jesus according to the thoughts of the bullies around Him was the ultimate scattering. After the scattering they would, of course, plan to kill the discipled Apostles. They have come to taunt Him in His final hours.

The *"strong bulls of Bashan"* have surrounded Jesus. Who are they? Why, dear friends, they are *"the chief priests, scribes, and elders."* These are Israel's religious leaders.

When a person thinks that their pastor doesn't care or doesn't have time for them that is one thing, but when the chief priest wants to KILL you; that's a major problem. Not only that, the mockery they were spewing was not that different than what Satan had said or would have said in the Wilderness

Temptations. When the priests are full of hell and the devil, what chance does a lamb who is counting on these religious leaders, really have?

The bulls were these evil people in authority, with power, with position and voice speaking through their bullhorns, taunting and mocking, striking their hooves against the ground as if they themselves wanted to charge the Son of God.

The commoners, the lay people would never have had enough gall to spit such at Jesus; after all, aside from His loyal Disciples and followers, many had been with Him in the multitudes and been taught, healed, fed. Only the evil men who wielded power would have been bold enough to say or inspire these things against Jesus. This is evidence of spiritual entities influencing humans to do evil.

If the *"bulls of Bashan"* were actually human, why does Psalms call them bulls and not people? These religious leaders are called *"bulls"* because they are operating under Satan's influence. They are corrupted and have allowed themselves to be used of the Devil. It is the goal of every idol, devil, or demon to have those that they are oppressed by to take on the nature of that demon. They have come to bully Jesus. Satan entered Judas, don't you think Satan or any of his devils or demons can enter your neighbor or your fake friends, or sneaky coworkers?

We don't war against flesh and blood, so we will pray to handle this in the spirit.

The Bulls of Bashan were big; Bashan was home to giants— enormous men—who were tools of Satan. This brings to mind the storybook legend of Paul Bunyan and Babe the Blue Ox, which was a massive bull. The giants of the Bible were known even from Genesis to defile humankind, especially the women and in so doing, keep the land polluted and make Israel intimidated as if seeing themselves as grasshoppers.

Like the giants of Bashan, Israel's religious leaders were also entered into by Satan to become defiling instruments against God's people and His land.

Then entered Satan into Judas surnamed Iscariot, being of the number of the twelve.

And he went his way, and communed with the chief priests and captains, how he might betray him unto them. (Luke 22:3-4)

Believing they had defeated Jesus; they mocked the Lord Jesus as He died for our sins--, and theirs, if you think about it. Christ in His passion, prayed that the Cup of Suffering might pass from Him; yet He capitulated to the Will of God.

Many bulls have compassed me - Men with the fierceness and fury of bulls. Saints of God, if you are seeing the signs of evil horns coming up against you, then you've been compassed about as well.

I was born and raised in the country; I think of the horns of bulls and how they are designed as weapons to gore enemies, predators, the rodeo performer or clown, and sometimes the negligent rancher. Strong bulls of Bashan refer also to wild bulls, not even the ones that have been reared on a ranch or those who have been as domesticated as possible. An ox is a castrated bull, so it is not as aggressive.

I believe the imagery of a bull was chosen in the Bible because of all the animals that have horns, (not antlers, but horns), bulls can have the biggest and toughest horns. Horns are alive and continue to grow as long as the animal is alive. Along with their aggression and territorial nature, we may see the worst combination in potentially attacking animals in the **bull**. Therefore, we see the worst possible traits in humans who have taken on the nature of the bull---, or the bully. And they are stubborn, so you know we've got to repent, pray, fast – and stand therefore until the battle is won.

The bulls in general, but especially those of Bashan are noted for their remarkable size, strength, and their fierceness. When used to describe men (who are bullies), they depict men that were fierce, savage, and violent. They are bullies, men who have assumed power or authority that surpasses that of the victim, or the would-be victim.

His enemies, with the vigor of bulls and rapacity of lions, surround him, eagerly sought His death; they had already tried to kill Him at least seven other times. Seeking after Jesus' life started as soon as He got here, before His ministry even started. Remember Herod wanted the Wise Men to come and tell him where the child was once they found Him.

Even though they did not, that didn't stop Herod, he just killed all the males 2 years and under in the land. That is **bully** behavior.

Bulls are territorial and violent. the chief priests, elders, Scribes, and Pharisees, among the Jews, and Herod and Pontius Pilate among the Gentiles, were compared to bulls for they too were guarding their territory. NO, they weren't protecting the people, they were protecting themselves and their positions – the territory that they ruled over. People didn't need protection **_from_** Jesus; they needed protection from the "spiritual leaders." Selah.

So if you are under attack by evil horns, THEY ARE NOT PLAYING WITH YOU.

From the time Jesus arrived here on Earth, some bull somewhere at some time was trying to push Him with their horns of power and authority. This was not just in the natural, Satan took Him up on a high place to tempt Him as well. Not to Jesus, but to any average person who is NOT in the spirit, that is a form of bullying because the devil is using spiritual power that must be answered with spiritual power or the Word of God, but if we don't know, we don't know. If we don't use that power, then a power can be exerted that makes it an unfair fight. Boxing gloves won't answer that kind of power.

But these Pharisees and the like, their desire was to trample Him, kill Him. They surrounded Him, apprehended Him, turned Him over to Pilate and He was condemned when they chose Barrabas over Jesus.

Many bulls have compassed me:
strong *bulls* of Bashan have beset me round.

`"Bulls and buffaloes are very numerous, says Canon Tristram, "in Southern Judaea; they are in the habit of gathering in a circle around any novel or unaccustomed object, and may be easily instigated into charging with their horns"

We must fight the *horns* and if they are personified or exemplified as bulls of Bashan then shall we also then use the same thing that Jesus fought them with? His Blood. The matadors in Spain may wave a red cape to incite the animals, but we can plead the red Blood of Jesus to defeat the spiritual *horns* that are sent or assigned to attack us, in the Name of Jesus.

Bully

Where does the term, *bully* come from?

It is supposed that the word, *bully* used to be a term of endearment, but then it became used as the protector of a prostitute. Perhaps this word was adopted from a Middle Dutch word, *boele*, and not bully, or anything having to do with a bull, at all. Plus, how do you protect someone who is in constant sexual sin? Only in the physical, and only by physical violence. The repercussions of the constant sin will be spiritual, and I've never heard of a spiritual *pimp*.

So, this word, ***bully*** might simply be derived from the noun ***bull***, **uncastrated male bovine animal**. This might be supported by the fact that the verb ***bullock***, which appeared in the early 18th century in the sense to bully (it now means to work long and hard), is from the noun *bullock*, which originally denoted a young bull, or bull calf. Working hard but not receiving or enjoying the fruit of your labor is another symptom of being under attack by evil *horns*. In the natural, what does the **bully** do? He takes lunches, lunch money, and whatever else he wants from his victim. See how that correlates to spiritual bullying?

Metaphorical bullying is too common, as is the bully too common; even one bully is too many. The "bully offer" is an extravagant and shady offer for a house. Theodore Roosevelt's bully pulpit speaks of the platform (or microphone) that a person can use to verbally attack others who have no platform, or microphone of their own to speak up for themselves or fight back. Some bad pastors are accused of using the pulpit as a bully pulpit.

Bully can mean teasing, rumor-spreading, harassing, abusing, coercing, online-terrorizing, torturing, slandering or maligning, marginalizing, offending, among other things. Spiritual *horns* intend to put reproach on their victim, which harasses, and marginalizes them in the natural.

As long as a bully thinks you're weak or you are a victim, or can become one, they will bully you or continue to bully you. Jesus was no victim, but the devil thought He was. Jesus had been downgraded to a slave by Judas and the thirty pieces of silver, to an idol *god* by being nailed to a tree (the Cross), to a mockery by the guards, and now the devil thought Jesus was defeated, and therefore a victim. Licking his chops, the devil probably thought Jesus was his victim and that the devil had won.

Not so. But even today people like to choose the team that they think will win, so vicariously they can feel like a winner. It looked like the devil had defeated the Son of God.

Not so. Not so.

But what was really happening in the spirit is that Jesus was a willing sacrifice, not a slave. Jesus worked for mankind, giving of Himself so that salvation would be free, especially since no mortal man could have been the perfect sacrifice. Jesus is the Son of

God, not an idol. In the spirit, Jesus was defeating Death; Jesus was the victor over Death, not a victim. Let those with eyes to see, see what the Lord was doing that day at Calvary.

A bully would never try to bully someone known to be greater, bigger, stronger, more powerful than himself. That wouldn't be bullying, that would be stupid. If evenly matched it would be a fair fight. But when a bully judges someone to be weak that's when they want to fight. A bully is a poor judge of people. He is one who just powers in and tries to steamroll over people. We do not know who is protecting any one of us in the Spirit---, until we know. Therefore, a bully won't know what power will arise to contend with, fight, or overcome the power that they are availing themselves to try to overcome us.

We all need God, 24/7; He is the greatest power.

Signs that Spiritual Horns are Warring Against You

Classically, the devil comes not but to steal kill and destroy. John 10:10 reads that the thief comes not but to steal kill and destroy. So, if you see thieving, stealing, killing, and destroying happening in your life, generally it is the devil. Specifically, you need to discern what division of evil the devil has sent against you. Has he sent evil *horns*?

The Holy Spirit helps our prayers, but we can be more effective if we call out what we are praying against. On deliverance ground there are *some* that will not come out unless you call them by name. So, know your enemy; that is also a very important rule of war.

Horns are an escalation from basic witchcraft attack and therefore repent of calling it to yourself if you have done this unknowingly. Repent of your ignorance of not knowing and then begin to take action against the horns.

Bulls are male bovines and are far more aggressive than cows. We were always taught as kids, to stay away from them. Bulls tend to be more territorial, have higher hormone levels, and are usually less socialized with humans than cows, and they are much larger and stronger. Bulls have HORNS. Some cows have horns, but the horns on bulls are larger and thicker. Some cows do not have horns, and some have been bred to be hornless, while ALL bulls have horns.

Signs that evil *horns* are working against you. Horns specialize in shedding blood. Loss. Scattering things, lives, families, marriages.

Are you having violent dreams? I was until I prayed the prayers in this book, then they stopped immediately. Violent dreams are a sign that there is a dream or sleep affliction and that something is wrong that you need to address. Horns want to scatter – if you're exhausted all day from dream afflictions all night then you might be what's called a scatterbrain at work all day. I'm not saying that just saying the word horns out of context, or in some vague context caused horns to be released against me, I just looked at the symptoms that I was experiencing to determine what might be the cause. Also, after praying against evil horns, the symptoms subsided or left me. Therefore, there was a connection. In addition to that, the Holy Spirit reminded me of my having sung that song over and again, even years ago.

The evil horns seek shame for you. They cause reproach to come upon you, people disdain you or hate you for no reason, even in your own family. Nobody wants to beg anyone to love them, but if you buy into that and also decide that you don't care because you think *they* don't care, you may find yourself isolated and that is what an abusive spouse wants; to isolate you. The devil is the abusive spouse; don't marry him. Please!

Under attack by evil horns? You may notice one or more of the following:

a. Patterns of loss and misfortune in your life.
b. Extreme work; little to no profit.
c. Failure at the edge of breakthrough. *Almost-there* syndrome.
d. Constantly harassed by something spiritual,-- evil powers, in the natural or your dream life.
e. Unexplained business failure. It is as though your hands are cursed, but they are not, are they?
f. Watching and even cheering for the success of others, waiting patiently for your turn. It's your turn, *right*?
g. Marital problems, for no real reason. The horns attack marriages, big time.
h. At the wrong church – again.
i. Fear for no real reason, agitation, on edge. There's a bull charging you in the spirit, no wonder you're on edge.
j. Picking the wrong romantic partners.
k. Wrong friends, fake friends, mischievous or evil friends who are trying to lead you into trouble.
l. Restless, but you don't know why.
m. Health issues--, if not you, someone in your household or family. That is still

designed to affect you, time, money…emotional worry, distraction from things you should be doing.

n. Spirit is willing but the flesh is weak? There is a power drawing you to do wrong, or to do nothing, to make you lazy and ineffective. God hates both.

Folks, this is another whole level above plain old witchcraft which you may have thought was a formidable opponent on its own. Well, if you don't do anything about it, it is powerful and may have its way in your life, except for God. Except for the Mercy of God.

Blow the Trumpet in Zion

Sound the trumpet for this warfare.

If that is what you mean, then say that. Sing that. Pray that. Do not leave words, which are weapons and can be weaponized hanging out there in the atmosphere for the devil to manipulate them against you or give himself a license to do something in your life that you never intended that he do.

Be specific when you speak. Be intentional; the devil is. In warfare we must be wiser and more strategic than our opponents.

How to Fight the Horns

How do you fight *horns*? Get yourself in order first. If the mighty have legal right to be in your life because of sin and iniquity, then they will just be there, attacking you, stealing, killing, destroying. So, get yourself right before God, first:

- Repent.
- Fast.
- Pray.

Okay, what do I pray?

When you pray you are using the same mouth that you may have used to either curse yourself or assist the enemy in getting a curse that he wanted to land against you to disappoint or devastate your life.

Your mouth is a weapon. Period. You must decide how you will use it day by day, hour by hour, minute by minute, really. If you don't know if you are the problem and causing your own problems, then be quiet, ask the Lord, and listen. If you know you are the problem, then do the same. Learn the Word of God--, even in verses and pieces and then begin to speak that instead of what you might normally say while frustrated or in your flesh.

Do not invite disaster into your life with your own words; the *boogie*, the singing, the song, even if it is your jam, is not worth it. So I sang a song every now and then for two or three years while in a rebellious, secular music phase and then it takes how many years to get rid of the spiritual problem that first, I didn't even know was a problem. Then I didn't know it was a spiritual problem. Then I didn't know how to pray about it. How much time has gone by to get out of something that I thought brought me entertainment, pleasure or passing joy? What has been lost in the process, besides time? What has been stolen? What has been killed? What has been destroyed?

Whatever it was, whether I ever know or not, it was NOT worth it.

Growing up, the old folks told us that rock and roll was devil music. Not just rock and roll. And can we say all music? I don't know, we need to ask the Lord. Whether the music has words or not we must consider the source, what or who inspired the song, and what *spirit* is being released with any song instrumental or not. What is the name of the song? Musicians love to be irreverent when they write, play and perform their music. Not only does it get them attention and acclaim, I believe it is a spiritual signature as to where they got the music and what "god" or gods they serve.

David came to the palace to play for King Saul to chill Saul out when he was demonized. So, music can drive demons out, but it seems music can drive demons into a person as well. None of us should be too quick to demonize other people's music while ignoring what we listen to, sing, or *boogie* to ourselves. It depends on the music and what *spirits* are involved in it or behind it.

It is said that 30 witches pray over secular music so that people will like it, buy it, and it will make money for the record label. This type of praying is not accidental, and they aren't praying to God. Further, the witches aren't doing this for free; if money is being exchanged then an evil covenant is made. The devil is in every evil deal, contract, or covenant.

What is in that song or any song that motivates the devil to anoint it? What's in it for the devil? He is the prince of the powers of the air, after all. He is not greater than God, but when it comes to anything of God, how many saints of God are getting together to pray over anything that we want released into the world or into the atmosphere? And if two or three are gathered, do they pray more than a 5-minute prayer one time and then decide okay, God did it, it is done. Let's sit back and watch TV now and let it happen.

TV---, another device used by the prince of the power of the air.

Divine Carpenters

Carpenters in Bible times worked with all kinds of materials. A divine carpenter was a spiritual being, of God and sent by God. We will talk sometimes about carpenters in the natural as well as in the spirit through this discourse.

So the **carpenter** encouraged the goldsmith, *and* he that smootheth *with* the hammer him that smote the anvil, saying, It *is* ready for the sodering: and he fastened it with nails, *that* it should not be moved. (Isaiah 41:7)

The **carpenter** stretcheth out *his* rule; he marketh it out with a line; he fitteth it with planes, and he marketh it out with the compass, and maketh it after the figure of a man, according to the beauty of a man; that it may remain in the house. (Isaiah 44:13)

> Is not this the **carpenter**, the son of Mary, the brother of James, and Joses, and of Juda, and Simon? and are not his sisters here with us? And they were offended at him.
> (Mark 6:3)

Its no mistake that God has divine carpenters in the Old Testament and His Only Begotten Son is known in the natural as the son of a carpenter.

> Is not this the carpenter's son? is not his mother called Mary? and his brethren, James, and Joses, and Simon, and Judas?
> (Matthew 13:55)

My maternal grandfather was a carpenter. It seems that in the Bible, although the word carpenter is only mentioned only about a dozen times, a carpenter was a pretty big deal back then. A carpenter could wield tools to pluck up, tear up, tear down and then build things back up again. Carpenter is first mentioned in 2 Samuel 5:11 and last mentioned in Zechariah 1:20 in the Old Testament.

Synonyms for carpenter include workman, craftsman, engraver, artificer, smith, maker. Not only could these carpenters efficiently use tools, they also could make the tools they used. They were called artisans, engravers. They were also skillful in being able to destroy warriors. They didn't just build houses. They were masons and could fabricate any material, according to Strong's H2790.

So, in the Book of Zechariah when God sent Divine Carpenters or Divine Craftsmen, that was no afterthought.

The KJV translates Strong's G5045 as following, among other definitions:

- a worker in wood, a carpenter, joiner, builder.
- a ship's carpenter or builder
- any craftsman, or workman
- a planner, contriver, plotter

A carpenter could work in stone, iron, and copper, as well as in wood. The tools used by carpenters are mentioned in several places in the Old Testament, 1 Samuel 13:19, Judges 4:21 and Isaiah 10:15, for example.

Spiritually, Jesus as a "carpenter" worked with **souls** and **spirits**--, people. It was said of our Lord, "Is not this the carpenter?" (Mark 6:3).

Every Jew, even the rabbis, had a vocation or learned a handicraft: Paul was a tentmaker. In the cities the carpenters would be Greeks. This is the same as in our day some people groups have a preponderance of skilled workers in whatever field they trade in. God made it that way. I'm amazed at how South Africans can sing. The work of tilers from Spain and Mexico is so beautiful. Online I see many from Slavic countries make beautiful wood products. This doesn't preclude others from doing the same, but I see a trend in certain countries or people groups. God intended it this way; if we all work together, everything we need would be available to all of us.

A carpenter is an artificer who works in timber, a framer and builder of houses, and of ships. Those who build houses are called house-carpenters, and those who build ships are called ship-carpenters. In New England, a distinction is often made between the man who frames, and the man who executes the interior woodwork of a house. The framer is the *carpenter* and the finisher is called joiner;

they are both still carpenters. In Italy and Spain, a carpenter is a coach-maker. No matter the distinctions or subcategories, a carpenter is well versed in using certain tools.

A carpenter is an artificer, he is a graver. He is a worker in metals. A carpenter could work in wood, and he could work with stone. *(See Appendix for Scripture references.)*

So, the Divine Carpenters that the Lord sends come to do a specific work and they have specific spiritual tools to do that job against the evil horns.

the craftsmen have come to terrify them and throw down these horns of the nations who lifted up their horns against the land of Judah to scatter its people." (Zechariah 1:21)

5. Lord, have Your Divine Carpenters terrify and throw down every evil horn, every nation that has lifted up its horn against me, in the Name of Jesus.
6. Lord, restore, redeem, renew, replenish, re-member and put me back together before the scattering, in the Name of Jesus.
7. Lord, remove all reproach from my life, in the Name of Jesus.

Men Skilled to Destroy

> I will pour out My indignation on you. I will blow on you with the fire of My fury. I will hand you over to brutal men, skilled to destroy. (Ezekiel 21:36 TLV)

Now we get to Ezekiel 21:36 where the definition changes to, *men skilled to destroy.* As this carpenter can work in metals and iron, shall he not also be able to forge weapons? Is he not the forerunner to the blacksmith and ironsmith? Beat plowshares into weapons? He is a skilled weapon maker and as well can be a skilled user of such weapons.

In many movies we see mighty warriors making their own weapons. No warrior is worth anything if he doesn't know his weapons.

> I will pour out my anger upon you, breathing my fiery wrath against you; I will hand you over to ravagers, artisans of destruction! (Ezekiel 21:36 NABRE)

73

Artisans of destruction--, sounds like Divine Carpenters to me. These Divine Carpenters are what we may think of as hit men. I'm sure they will not miss their mark. As God chooses the foolish to confound the wise, we humans might think He would send in a Divine Horn to fight a demonic horn. He's God; He does as He pleases. He steps this up and sends in Divine Carpenters to terrify the horns and scatter that which was sent to scatter.

As a carpenter is anointed to work with wood and other metals and the Cross that Jesus was crucified on was made of wood, and it was the plan of God that He should be hung on it, can we not think that Divine Carpenters built that Cross, or men under divine auspices built it? I don't believe God sent in Divine Carpenters **after** Jesus was already on the Cross because the Cross was constructed by them. Surely. But we mere men wait until the drama starts or unfolds before we call for help from the Sanctuary.

Not Jesus. Not God. Golgotha was already planned; the Lamb was slain **before** the world was formed.

That Old Rugged Cross was made of wood, and carpenters are skilled to work with wood. Trees, obviously where wood comes from, were a place of illicit worship, and unfortunately, they still are. One of the reasons Jesus was put on that wooden Cross, is that "tree" was a sort of proclamation that He was not Who He really was, and it was a declaration that those who worshipped Him were not worshipping their own "God", but instead they tried to reduce Christ to an object of idol worship. We know Jesus is not an idol, but evil leaders are ever trying to deceive people to insure their own positions and power.

They tried to first reduce Jesus to a slave by Judas selling Him for 30 pieces of silver, then to a criminal, as criminals were hung on trees and in gallows, and crucified on crosses. Then they tried to reduce Him to an idol (a tree idol) by putting Him on a "tree." This was absolute mockery in that Jesus was the son of a carpenter. While at the same time a DIVINE CARPENTER could defeat them all. *Selah.*

The Lifter of My Head

I asked, "What are these coming to do?"

He answered, "These are the horns that
scattered Judah so that no one could raise
their head, but the craftsmen have come to
terrify them and throw down these horns of
the nations who lifted up their horns against
the land of Judah to scatter its people."
(Zechariah 1:19-21)

Lord, how are they increased that trouble
me! many are they that rise up against me.

Many there be which say of my soul, There is
no help for him in God. Selah.

But thou, O Lord, art a shield for me; my
glory, and the lifter up of mine head. (Psalm
3:1-3)

Head down, feet shuffling, despondent,
isolated, alone, feeling forlorn, depressed or
hopeless is not of God. When we feel
depressed or defeated the head automatically
goes down. This could be the work of evil
horns.

I am troubled; I am bowed down greatly; I go mourning all the day long. (Psalm 38:6)

When a person is captive, they may be bowed down or pressed down. A person's head could be down because of guilt as they are lying down in sin, in polluted blood. The captured soul may be depressed and forlorn. This *capturing* is a spiritual phenomenon that is described as one's *head* being captured. How can a head be captured?

- Evil and trigger dreams.
- Evil summons.
- Evil touch.
- Evil exchange.
- Masquerade /evil veil/ evil covering.
- Incision (tattoos are so dangerous), but there are spiritual tattoos that you cannot even see.
- Evil marks.
- Sleeping with demonic, wicked, occultic, humans or others–, every person is not necessarily a *human*.
- Evil barber/backbiting/evil hairdresser/ demonic hair products.
- Trauma/traumatic brain injury.

- Foremost, constant attack by spiritual bulls and natural bullies will cause a head to be down.

He answered, "These are the horns that scattered Judah so that no one could raise their head, but the craftsmen have come to terrify them and throw down these horns of the nations who lifted up their horns against the land of Judah to scatter its people." (Zechariah 1:20-21)

When a person feels that they just don't have the strength or the ability to get it together and rise up and move forward in life, it is because of evil horns. It is because of the horns that bully, that intimidate, that scatter.

When a nation cannot again rise because their horn, their power, or their authority has been removed, destroyed or scattered, that is a sign of evil horns having attacked or overtaken them.

Internal fighting can cause this kind of destruction as well. Animals with horns use their horns against one another if they are wild, untamed, predatory, evil, vying for dominance, and or have no defined leader. There was a study done years ago that showed that if there is not a proper leader of a pack of elephants, then the teen, male elephants will act out. So, it goes with people as well.

My God of Mercy, when you feel or know that you've got so much working against you in life and here come people, actual or supposed human beings to attack you or tear you down further, it can feel like too much. Especially when these people are relatives, friends, or those you have trusted with your secrets. We must pray before trusting to let the Holy Spirit lead us into friendships, relationships, and alliances. Amen.

For innumerable evils have compassed me about: mine iniquities have taken hold upon me, so that I am not able to look up; they are more than the hairs of mine head: therefore my heart faileth me. (Psalm 40:12)

There could be other reasons the head is down. For instance, the carnal man is narcissistic, looking down at himself, checking himself out all day.

Prayers for Deliverance of the Head:

8. Lord, locate me, by the power in the Blood of Jesus. Locate my head, in Jesus' Name.

9. My destiny, be unlocked and uncaged, in the Name of Jesus.

10. Household and *familiar spirit* witchcraft, fail against me, in the Name of Jesus.

11. Lord, if I come from a bloodline of captured minds, souls, or heads, I repent for myself and my ancestors. Lord, forgive all sin, remove iniquity and remove this curse from my family bloodline, in the Name of Jesus.

12. If my spouse comes from a foundation of captivity, especially of the head, LORD, remove this curse from their foundation that our family may live and thrive, in the Name of Jesus.

13. I bind the work of every backbiting evil hairdresser and barber against me, and my spouse and family, in the Name of Jesus.

14. Holy Spirit, show me demonic haircare products, processes, and styles, so that I may remove and destroy them today, in the Name of Jesus.

15. Evil touch on my head; I break your power by the Power in the Blood of Jesus.

16. Backbiting, evil pronouncements upon my life, lose your power over me; I break your curse, in the Name of Jesus.

17. All my glory stolen from me from birth until now, I command you to return to me, in the Name of Jesus; Lord deal with the thief or thieves involved in taking my glory, in the Name of Jesus.

18. Evil mark and every mark of failure, Blood of Jesus, blot it off me and out of my life, in the Name of Jesus.

19. My crown of good success, return to me now, in the Name of Jesus.

20. Covering cast, evil veil, masquerade hiding my head, catch Fire and be removed from my head forever, in the Name of Jesus.

21. Lord, let my destiny helpers and all divine connections find me now, in the Name of Jesus. Demonic cages hiding my true identity blocking my helpers from reaching me, I command you to break completely, in Jesus' Name.

22. Evil summons, I will not answer you, I will not obey your evil instructions, by the power in the Blood of Jesus.

23. Any demonic hand touching me, pressing my head down, saying I shall not rise, you are a liar; I shall rise—you fall down and die, in the Name of Jesus.

24. All rejection in my life, turn to favor and celebration now, in the Name of Jesus.

25. I receive full deliverance from my head by Fire, in Jesus' Name. *(adapted from the book: **Anatomy of Deliverance** by Stephen Beloved)*

One's head could be down because you have little or no self-esteem – do not know who you are? You may have been lied to about who you are. You may have been disrespected for so long that you think you are what *they* say about you. You may think that you are what you've been through.

26. You can only know who you are <u>in</u> Christ. No one else will either know or tell you the truth of your identity.

27. Lord, if I am none of Yours give me Godly sorrow for my sins, receive my repentance, and make me one of Yours, in the Name of Jesus.

Knowing what God says about you and knowing the Word of GOD will **lift your head**.

- Foremost you are created in the image and likeness of God: Lift up your head.
- You are created a little lower than the Angels (the Elohim) Lift up your head.

- You are CROWNED WITH GLORY AND HONOR: LIFT UP YOUR HEAD—how will your crown stay on with your head bowed down.
- This day, I have begotten thee, says the Lord, thou art My son, forever: lift up your head.
- You are accepted in the Beloved, lift up your head.
- You are set in dominion with authority; LIFT UP YOUR HEAD.
- The wicked will not rule forever: LIFT UP YOUR HEAD

Do you feel or know that you've been left for dead, by the side of the road or in your own blood: the head is lifted to give air, such as in CPR: with all that is within you, lift up your head.

28. LORD breathe life into me again—breathe new life into me, in the Name of Jesus.
29. LIFT UP MY HEAD, LORD, Give me spiritual CPR, in the Name of Jesus.

The head is lifted to look into the eyes of a person – thy face Lord, I will seek. When thou saidst, Seek ye my face; my heart said unto thee, Thy face, Lord, will I seek. (Psalm 27:8)

30. LORD, look on me. Let your countenance shine upon me. Lord, be Gracious unto me and give me Peace.

When someone is talking to you, it is only natural that you will look up to see who is speaking, who is addressing you. If you are talking to God, He will be talking to you. El Roi, the God who sees me, He is the lifter of my head.

How many news reports have you seen where a perp is being arrested and the first thing he does is drop his head? Many perps try to hide or cover their head. This is guilt, of course. You don't have sin guilt, do you? HAVE YOU BOWED TO IDOLS? HAVE YOU BOWED TO SATAN? HAVE YOU BOWED TO THE FLESH? Have you bowed down your head willingly and now you can't lift it up because those idols are still demanding their worship??? Sin and its guilt are things that make the work of evil *horns* against you very easy. Sin is ever opening doors to Satan.

We don't serve a God that we will be ashamed of and He will not leave us in shame. Secret Christians were in the Bible, and even now. For thought: was Nicodemus worse than Peter who denied Jesus three times in one night?

The Word says: **My people shall never be ashamed.**

And ye shall know that I am in the midst of Israel, and that I am the Lord your God, and none else: and **my people shall never be ashamed.** (Joel 2:27)

One must lift his head to see where he is going, if he is going anywhere in life. One with his head down is either not moving or going nowhere in life. With the head down we cannot see where we are going, or we only go on a pre-set path.

If the head doesn't lift the rest of the body will not lift. Have you noticed that in many deliverance services, the deliverance minister will say to the person they are ministering to: LOOK AT ME?

If the enemy captures your head, he has captured 7 of the 9 GATES of your body.

In your *feels, when* the mind is captured: a person may feel depressed, forgetful, hurt,

- Prayer life has dried up.
- Mind wandering.
- Sleep wave.
- Severe unexplainable headaches.
- Blank mind;
- Brain fog,
- Forgetfulness.—senior moments. I've told you that senior moments are not to be laughed at or accepted; it is a demonic phenomenon, possibly because of the head being captured.
- Confusion/ lack of concentration, especially when reading the Bible.
- Feeling things crawling or moving in your head? Have you been eating in the dream in the past and haven't dealt with it?
- Dream afflictions—crazy dreams and nightmares almost every night.
- Evil visions as soon as you close your eyes.
- Feeling controlled.
- Seeing dead people in your dreams or even hallucinations in the daytime.

- Thoughts of the dead, thoughts of death or suicide. **THOSE ARE NOT YOUR THOUGHTS! THAT IS DEMONIC. THAT IS DEMONS ON ASSIGNMENT TRYING TO DRIVE YOU NUTS, YES, BUT ALSO TRYING TO GET YOU TO AGREE WITH THEIR DEATH PROGRAM FOR YOUR LIFE, OR DO NOTHING ABOUT WHAT THEY ARE SENDING TO YOU SO BY DOING NOTHING YOU AGREE WITH THEM.**
- **With the breath of life that God gives us comes the will to live. It is why we breathe automatically. It is why we get hungry regularly and eat. The will to live is why we avoid pain. Anything else is demonic. Thoughts of death are not your thoughts!**

Prayers:

31. I cast down every evil imagination that exalts itself against the knowledge of God, in the Name of Jesus.
32. Every thought, image and word of death, I bind you and cast you out of my mind and

out of my heart, now, in the Name of Jesus. Go! Go! Go! You must go, in the Name of Jesus.

33. Every thought, image, or word of suicide or hopelessness, I bind you and cast you and every demon promoting such an attack against me, out out, out, in the Name of Jesus.

34. Every curse of personal destruction or suicide sent to me from any origin at any time, from any entity or evil human agent, lose your power, and leave my life now, in the Name of Jesus.

35. Every spiritual attack against my correct identity in God, I reject you now, in the Name of Jesus.

36. Every spiritual attack that causes my head to lower or hang down, I break your power over me by the power in the Blood of Jesus.

37. I vomit out all *spiritual* food and beverage eaten in the dream, in the Name of Jesus.

38. I reverse all damage done to me because of evil spirit food, in the Name of Jesus.

39. Night caterers of evil spiritual food fed to me, forced on me, or given to me in the dream, I reject all *spiritual* food and beverage, I reject you, eat your own food,

drink your own beverage and fall down and die, in the Name of Jesus.

40. Anything implanted or moving in my head, or anywhere in my body because of evil spiritual food, come out, come out, come out now, with all your roots, and have no effect on me, by the power in the Blood of Jesus.

41. I shall live. I shall live. I shall live. I shall live and not die, and declare the goodness of the Lord, in the Name of Jesus.

42. I shall live until I am satisfied, and in divine health, godly health, perfect health, vitality, vigor and in prosperity, in the Name of Jesus.

43. Every masquerade keeping me in grief, excessive grief, or pulling me down to the grave, by the power in the Blood of Jesus I command you to leave my dreams, my life, my mind and my consciousness, in the Name of Jesus.

44. My deceased loved ones are in the arms of the Lord God, they are not with me, visiting me, or talking to me. According to the Word of God, the dead know nothing, in the Name of Jesus.

45. I will not be drawn to the grave, or be a victim of untimely death, in the Name of Jesus.
46. I shall live until I am satisfied, and in divine health, godly health, perfect health, vitality, vigor and in prosperity, in the Name of Jesus.

Anger is one of the most common signs of captivity. Your head may not be down, but it is not in the right position if you are in constant anger, arrogance, or pride.

Pride comes before the fall.

Adam & Eve took food from the serpent who fell from heaven, like lightning, because of pride. What happened to Adam & Eve next? They fell from their God-created positions and lost their home, their paradise.

Reject *spirit* food, no matter what it is called – an apple? Reject food from the prideful – pride comes before the fall.

Physical signs of captivity:
- Worry and anxiety
- Excessive worry,
- Tension, irritation.

- Problems appear HUGE and they may not be.
- On edge.
- Restless.
- Muscle tension and aches.
- Headaches of any kind.
- Confusion.
- Sweating.
- Nausea/ indigestion.
- Frequent bathroom breaks.
- Exhaustion/tiredness.
- Fidgeting—no Peace.
- Can't sleep. Can't fall asleep. Can't stay asleep.

I cried unto the Lord with my voice, and
he heard me out of his holy hill. Selah.
I laid me down and slept; I awaked; for
the Lord sustained me.
I will not be afraid of ten thousands of
people, that have set themselves against
me round about.
Arise, O Lord; save me, O my God: for
thou hast smitten all mine enemies upon
the cheek bone; thou hast broken the teeth
of the ungodly.

Salvation belongeth unto the Lord: thy
blessing is upon thy people. Selah. (Psalm
3: 4-8)

- Tremors, trembling
- Easily startled/unsettled.
- Numb hands and feet.
- Difficulty swallowing.
- Breathing difficulty (sporadic).
- Twitching.
- Hot flashes.
- Hives/rashes.

Many of these are signs of witchcraft attack
as well—I go over that at length in my book:
Upgrade: How to Get Out of Survival Mode.

Prayers:

47. Lord, help me. I command every negative
    spiritual projection into my mind, soul, and
    life to be uprooted and burned to ashes,
    now, in the Name of Jesus.
48. Every witchcraft attack, back to sender, in
    the Name of Jesus.
49. *Spirits* of confusion and uncertainty, you
    are bound by the power in the Name of
    Jesus and cast out of my life forever.

50. Lord, restore and repair all damage done to my spirit, soul, and body by demonic attacks that have come against my head and mind, in the Name of Jesus.
51. I bind and cast out the *spirit of fear* for the LORD has not given me the *spirit of fear*, but one of LOVE, power, and a sound mind, in the Name of Jesus, Amen.
52. Every evil and demonic imagination in the heart of evil human persecutors who have arisen against me and my family, I cast them down and bring them to nothing by the power in the Blood of Jesus.
53. My body, soul and spirit, resist the imaginations of self and of others, in the Name of Jesus.
54. Lord, cleanse my head from every evil thought, in the Name of Jesus.
55. Let the words of my mouth and the meditation of my heart be acceptable to you, my Lord, my strength and my Redeemer, in the Name of Jesus.

Lift up ye heads oh ye gates.

The head is a gate, and it has many gates. The body is compared to a city consisting of 9 gates (entrance/exits). Two eyes, two ears, your mouth, your nostrils, your anus and genitals.

Lift up your heads oh ye gates:

56. <u>Mouth</u>: Oh taste and see that the Lord is good.

Even in the natural some foods and beverages are demonic. Looking at the packaging may be a clue, it may not be... yes, these things are bewitched so they will be popular and sell a lot – just like music. *The mouth is a GATE, what you put in there determines what comes out.*

Jesus said it is not what a man puts in his mouth that defiles him, but what comes out. What you eat determines the health of your body – health or disease is what will come out – that is be the result of what you eat. **Isn't this why we pray and bless food before consumption in the natural?**

57. <u>Eyes</u>: I look past the hills from whence cometh my help, my help comes from the Lord.
58. Thy Face Lord, I will seek.

<u>Ears</u>: Faith comes by hearing.

Nostrils: And God breathed in him the *Breath of Life* and he became a living soul. What you breathe in can affect you or capture you. the latest is evil perfumes, colognes and fragrances. Don't get me started, but every fragrance is not safe or wise to use. Where they have been created and what is in them, and whether or not they have been demonically incanted over – enchanted is for you to pray and ask the Holy Spirit. Should I use this fragrance? Where did it come from? What, if anything has been done to it? What is in it? **You'd better know.**

False pastors—, evil marine pastors are known to use fragrances and perfumes to take dominion over your nose gates. Any gate – once they're in, they are in.

Saints of GOD, every time you smell pizza you've got to eat. Every time you smell chocolate or cake, or coffee or donuts, or whatever your weakness is, you have to eat every time you go past the bakery window or smell what they are cooking. If so, the enemy has control over your nose gates.

59. Instead, declare: I will have dominion over the enemy at the gates:

I don't mean to be too graphic, but the other gates are sexual, the reproductive and anal gates. Wouldn't you think the enemy wants to possess those gates as well? Whatever gate, whatever you let in--, is in there. Not only that, somehow it is addictive and you either want it again and again, or you are made or stimulated to believe you want it again.

That is until you hit rock bottom and can't take it anymore. Pray that that will happen before it is too late to do anything about it.

Under Judgment?

Are you under judgment from God? Then your head will be cast down for sure. He promised us dominion over our enemies, that we would possess the gates of the enemy, but if we are under judgment, then the opposite will be true.

Are you under judgment from God? Is that why your head is cast down? Ask Him. What have you done? What do you need to repent of? What do you need to make right again? Repent if you are the reason your head is cast down.

If what you are going through is not your doing, pray. Enter into spiritual battle and warfare. With God, you will win every time, if you stay with it until the end. Warfare is not always a one and done deal. There is not always a formula; pray until something happens, you pray until you get relief, release, and victory. Pray until the Spirit of God lets you know that it is done, and you don't need to pray about that anymore.

Not only will the Lord bring you out, but he will exalt you. He will not just lift your head, He will LIFT **YOU**.

When the LORD exalts your HEAD that means that the leadership of your life has both defeated and also now reigns over your enemies. The leadership of your life is what governs your life. A *lifted* leadership and governance is desired. Jesus should be the head of your life.

When the righteous are in authority, the people rejoice: but when the wicked beareth rule, the people mourn. (Proverbs 29:2)

When a man's ways please the Lord, even his enemies will be at peace with him.

Lifting means lifting your headship or your authority, your conditions in your life. O Lord, you are the lifter of my head. Amen.

60. I will **lift** up **my eyes** to the hills [of Jerusalem]— From where shall **my** help come? (Psalm 121:1)

"**Lift** up your **eyes** to the heavens, (Isaiah 51:6)

61. Declare: I will lift up my soul – emotions, will, and intellect. I will think on *better* things than I used to. I will have well-

ordered emotions. I will improve, better, and lift up my soul to the LORD. No matter what the situation or the conditions, I will walk upright before the LORD, no matter what others are doing.

62. I will lift up my voice and declare what the LORD says to declare (Isaiah 58:1)

"Cry aloud, do not hold back; Lift up your voice like a trumpet, And declare to My people their transgression And to the house of Jacob their sins.

Saints of God, when your head is raised up there is a boldness in what you speak. Yes, especially when it is from the Lord. We do what the Lord tells us, and we will speak the Word with authority and boldness.

63. I will lift up my voice in praise
64. I will lift up my hands in total praise to you
65. As I lift up my hands and heart toward Your innermost sanctuary (Holy of Holies). Psalm 28:2
66. For You are the LORD, the lifter of my head, the lifter of my LIFE. AMEN. None of the lifting of eyes, ears, heart, soul, hands in praise can happen with the head cast down.

They also that seek after my life lay
snares *for me*: and they that seek my
hurt speak mischievous things, and
imagine deceits all the day long. (Psalm 38:12)

Looking down looking for the traps set
for you; leery, worried about being trapped all
the time – paranoid could be a result of sin
guilt. You know you did wrong, you haven't
repented, so you just waiting for trouble. Why
not repent and pray instead?

When you realize that is death and hell
calling you, calling your name which is why
you keep looking down. LIFT UP YOUR
HEAD, do not answer Death, do not answer
the GRAVE, do not answer hell and do not give
them worship by looking down.

When the Lord orders your steps and
directs your path, when the Lord lights your
path, when the Lord makes crooked ways
straight, you don't have to worry about traps,
and snares, and nets, and falling.

In God you can lift up your head and
walk with confidence, you can walk and not be
weary, you can run your race, you will not be
stagnated; you can run on and see what the end
will be. LIFT UP YOUR HEAD.

Be pleased, O LORD, to deliver me: O LORD, make haste to help me. (Psalm 40:13)

Jesus said, If I be lifted up from the Earth, I will draw all men unto me. And I, if I be lifted up from the earth, will draw all men unto me. (John 12:32) – Jesus may have been speaking of His crucifixion, but we celebrate Jesus' Ascension and He is lifted up – high and lifted up, seated in heavenly places at the right hand of the Father. Amen.

GOD is the Lifter of my head, if Jesus is lifted up and I keep my eyes on Him then my head is lifted also.

- If I keep my eyes on Him, versus just looking at myself, my feelings, my needs, my wants, my head will be lifted and not cast down.
- If I keep my eyes on Him, versus my feet shuffling along the same old path day after day,
- If I keep my eyes on Him, versus listening to voices and influences that try to pull me down to the Earth, to hell…

- If I keep my eyes on Him instead of what men are doing, what man is doing – I will not fear what man can do to me.
- I lift mine eyes past the hills from whence cometh my help

67. My help comes from the LORD. If I keep my eyes on HIM, HE will lift my head and He will sustain me. Behold, God is my helper *and* ally; The Lord is the **sustainer** of my soul. (Psalm 54:4)

68. I bow down to worship the LORD GOD.

69. I BOW MY HEAD IN PRAYER.

70. I do not bow to idols.

71. I do not bow to false *gods*.

72. I do not bow to men who believe themselves to be God, I only bow down to worship Jehovah God.

73. The Lord is the lifter of my head and the sustainer of my soul. Amen.

Psalm 54:1-7

Save me, O God, by Your name;
And vindicate me by Your [wondrous] power.
Hear my prayer, O God;
Listen to the words of my mouth.
For strangers have risen against me
And violent men have sought my life;
They have not set God before them. Selah.
Behold, God is my helper *and* ally;
The Lord is the sustainer of my soul [my
upholder].
He will pay back the evil to my enemies;
In Your faithfulness destroy them.
With a freewill offering I will sacrifice to
You;
I will give thanks *and* praise Your name, O
LORD, for it is good.
For He has rescued me from every trouble,
And my eye has looked *with*
satisfaction (triumph) on my enemies.

Their mouth is an open sepulchre. Do
not let your mouth be a grave, speaking only of
death and defeat and giving evil reports
always. If you do, it is an indication of what is
in your heart because out of the heart the mouth
speaks.

Pray for deliverance of both your heart (soul) and mouth, in the Name of Jesus.

Lord, let my head be lifted up in victory.

74. Depart from me, all ye workers of iniquity; for the LORD hath heard the voice of my weeping.
75. The LORD hath heard my supplication; the LORD will receive my prayer.
76. Let all mine enemies be ashamed and sore vexed: let them return *and* be ashamed suddenly. (Psalm 6:8-10)

When you receive deliverance, your head will be raised, lift up—the Lord is the lifter of our heads because He is our deliverer from all captivity.

Lift up your head for this spiritual warfare for the Lord will give you the nations – all the evil that rose up against you:

Ask of Me, and I will give You The nations for Your inheritance, And the ends of the earth for Your possession. You shall break them with a rod of iron; You shall dash them to pieces like a potter's vessel. (Psalms 2:7-12 NKJV)

Divine Axe of the Lord

"You *are* My   battle-ax *and* weapons of   war:
For with you I will break the nation in pieces;
With   you   I   will   destroy   kingdoms;
With you I will break in pieces the horse and
its rider; With you I will break in pieces the
chariot and its rider; With you also I will
break   in   pieces   man   and   woman;
With you I will break in pieces old and young;
With you I will break in pieces the young man
and the maiden; (Jeremiah 51:20-26)

In Christianity, the Divine Axe of the
Lord is a weapon from His armory. It
symbolizes divine judgment and the cutting
away of what is unproductive or contrary to
God's purposes. It also serves as a reminder of
the need for repentance. From my book, **No**

Weapon Formed, we learned that we are designed to be weapons of God to be used against the enemy. As God calls us His battle-ax and weapons of war, we surely have to become that. We are born as babies and reborn as Christian babes in Christ, so we submit to the process and learn the Word of God and practice the disciplines of the Faith. We must get ready, stay ready, remain sharp.

Recently I had a dream where some entity asked me to give him my gun. Of course, I refused, but get your weapons ready, saints of God and do not relinquish them; do not let them go, and do not be tricked out of them. Most of us have watched enough or too many horror movies to know what a battle axe can do to the enemy; we are the Lord's battle-ax.

Is this not the perfect time, once you're ready to defeat the strongholds and strongmen of your bloodline. Is this not the perfect time to break the curses in your family? Can God use you? Can God trust you? Then do it.

Divine Scroll of God

In Zechariah 1:7-6:8, , the prophet Zechariah receives multiple visions; eight in total. They are listed with a brief description. We will discuss each in more details later in this chapter as well as have prayers related to the visions and our own deliverance which we seek from the Lord.

- The horseman among the myrtle trees (Zechariah 1:7-17)
- The four horns and four craftsmen (Zechariah 1:18-21).
- The surveyor (Zechariah 2:1-13).
- The vision of Joshua the high priest (Zechariah 3:1-10).
- The golden lampstand and two olive trees (Zechariah 4:1-14).
- The flying scroll (Zechariah 5:1-4).

- The woman in the basket (Zechariah 5:5-11).

- The four chariots (Zechariah 6:1-8).

This book of the Bible begins with a call for repentance (Zechariah 1:1-6). Each vision further emphasizes the need for repentance, which we must all do. It is good for man to repent. Daily, if not more than once daily.

77. Lord, have Mercy on me, a sinner. If I am none of Yours, make me one of Yours and give me Godly sorrow for my sin. Forgive me of all sins, transgressions, and iniquity. As well forgive the iniquity of my parents and my ancestors going all the way back to Adam and Eve where I retrieve my essence and my glory. Lord, restore me to my first estate, in the Name of Jesus. Amen.

This prophetic Book of the Bible is about God's plans for Israel and the coming of the Messiah. But are you not part of Israel? Are you not in Abraham? Are you part of the Body of Christ? Then we all too should be encouraged by the words of Prophet Zechariah as he speaks on the rebuilding of the Temple.

Is your body not the Temple of the Holy Spirit? Does your body not need to be built up, daily?

What? know ye not that your body is the temple of the Holy Ghost which is in you, which ye have of God, and ye are not your own? (1 Corinthians 6:19)

Doesn't your spirit man need to be edified and built up, daily?

But ye, beloved, building up yourselves on your most holy faith, praying in the Holy Ghost, (Jude 20).

Then find yourself and your encouragement in this Word of God.

Now let's look at the eight visions that the Lord gave the Prophet Zechariah.

One: The horseman among the myrtle trees (1:7-17): Zechariah sees a man and horses among the trees. The man explains that they had gone throughout the whole earth and found peace. An angel then tells the prophet that God still loved Israel and would restore Jerusalem.

"This is what the LORD Almighty says: 'My towns will again overflow with prosperity, and the LORD will again comfort Zion and choose Jerusalem.'"

78. Lord, send Your horsemen throughout my life, and anywhere You do not find peace, arise and contend with the enemies of my peace and my possessions, in the Name of Jesus.

Two: The four horns and four craftsmen (1:18-21): Zechariah is shown four horns and four craftsmen. The angel tells him that the horns are four kingdoms that opposed Israel (Assyria, Egypt, Babylon, and Medo-Persia) and the craftsmen (carpenters) are coming to "throw down these horns."

79. Lord, in the Name of Jesus any horns that are attacking my life, my destiny, my health, family, business, or career, send Your Craftsmen to deal with them. Defeat all the enemies against my life.

Three: The surveyor (2:1-13): Zechariah sees a man holding a measuring line. When the prophet asks the man where he is going, the man says he is going to measure the city of Jerusalem. God' is keeping His promise to expand Jerusalem, and its people will live in safety as the Lord judges Israel's enemies.

80. Lord, have Your surveyor measure my life, my reach, my influence, and my territory and enlarge my territory, my ministry, my influence, my abundance and let me live in safety all to the praise of Your Glory, in the Name of Jesus.

Four: The vision of Joshua the high priest (3:1-10): Zechariah sees Joshua standing before the Angel of the Lord in filthy clothes. Satan stands to the side to accuse the High Priest, Joshua. Folks this confirms that the Accuser of the Brethren is ever there when sins are committed to accuse and hopefully get God to Judge His creation--, us. But Jesus came to redeem mankind back to God. Satan is rebuked, and Joshua is given rich, clean clothes.

This vision of Joshua ends with a foretelling of the ultimate high priest, Jesus Christ, our coming Messiah, symbolized by a Branch and an all-seeing Stone.

81. Lord, redeem me by the Blood of the Lamb, in the Name of Jesus.
82. Lord, if I am in a wrong garment or a filthy garment, or being accused of such, change my garment, in the Name of Jesus.

Five: The golden lampstand and two olive trees (4:1-14): An angel shows Zechariah a golden lampstand being fed oil from two olive trees. The golden lampstand represents the temple and temple-worshiping community. God was making the point that He would once again work through His people to lay the foundation of the temple and finish the work.

83. Lord, do not remove Your lampstand from my life; receive my worship, let my worship be pleasing to you. Pour out fresh anointing on me daily; empower me to do Your Will and the work of ministry so that I may reach destiny, in the Name of Jesus.

Six: The flying scroll (5:1-4): Zechariah sees a large scroll, written on both sides, flying over the whole land. This vision speaks of God's judgment upon those who disobeyed His law.

"Again I lifted up my eyes and saw before me a flying scroll. 'What do you see?' asked the angel who was speaking with me. 'I see a flying scroll,' I replied, 'twenty cubits long and ten cubits wide.'" (Zechariah 5:1-2)

84. Lord, as with the scroll that the Prophet Zechariah saw, let Your divine law be the judge against the enemies of my soul. Let every horn up against me be judged by Your righteousness, in the Name of Jesus.

85. Lord, as Jesus took captivity captive, make a public show of defeating the horns that have arisen against me and let me be shown to be righteous according to the Blood of Jesus. Let me be vindicated. Let me be restored, back to my first estate or even better, in the Name of Jesus

86. Lord, as You judged the Chaldeans and the Amorites when their iniquity was full, let this be a full Judgment against the horns that have arisen up against Your child, in Jesus' Name.

87. Father, let Your judgment be swift and unavoidable against the *horns* that have arisen against me, in the Name of Jesus.

"This is the curse that is going out over the face of all the land, for according to what is written on one side, every thief will be banished, and according to what is written on the other side, everyone who swears falsely will be banished. I will send it out, declares the LORD of Hosts, and it will enter the house of the thief and the house of him who swears falsely by My name. It will remain inside his house and consume it, with its timber and stones." (Zechariah 5:3-4)

88. Lord, let Your Judgment destroy the houses of the horns up against me, even down to the timbers, in the Name of Jesus.

89. Lord, let Your flying Scroll, the judgment of the Lord chase the evil horns, in the Name of Jesus.

90. Lord, just as Your Word is sharper than a two-edged sword, let the two-sided message of Your Scroll address sins and all violations against You . Lord, by the presence of Your Scroll let Your law be active, pervasive, mighty and inescapable by the evil *horns*, in Jesus' Name.

91. Lord, I repent and renounce all sin. Lord, I pray for Mercy as You let Your Holiness and Justice pervade and prevail as You remove these evil horns from my life, by Your Divine Judgment, in the Name of Jesus.

92. Lord, by Your Spirit just as You helped the Israelites who were returning from Babylon, as I also return from my own sin, help me to rebuild my life everywhere it needs to be rebuilt, to Your specifications and praise from all that the evil horns have

taken of mine or destroyed, in the Name of Jesus.

93. Lord, redeem the time, restore the years; restore me to where I should be at this time in my life if I had never been attacked, oppressed, stolen from, hurt, deceived, or tricked by the enemy, in the Name of Jesus.

94. Lord, redeem the time, restore the years, place and establish me to where I would have been in my life if I had never sinned, and if my parents and ancestors had never sinned, and there was no iniquity to bear in my bloodline, in the Name of Jesus.

Seven: The woman in the basket (Zechariah 5:5-11).

95. Lord, I repent for my own sins and ask Mercy, in the name of Jesus. I call for Your judgment upon all Your enemies, especially those that have come up against me. Diminish and disgrace the powers, principalities, spiritual wickedness and rulers of darkness that are contending with me, in the Name of Jesus.

96. Lord, any iniquity or sin debt from any source in my life, my own sin, the sins of my parents or ancestors that is negatively

affecting my life, by the Blood of Jesus, forgive me, forgive my own bloodline, in the Name of Jesus.

97. Remove all iniquity from my foundation; remember it no more, in the Name of Jesus.

98. Father, any dark power or spiritual entity that has my life imprisoned in any vessel, a basket, cauldron, pot, jar or cage, send Your Angels to release me, in the Name of Jesus.

99. Any wickedness up against me that is hiding, Lord, just as Your angels took away the basket of wickedness in Zechariah's vision, have Your angels search them out, find them and take them away from my life, permanently, in the Name of Jesus.

Eight: The four chariots (Zechariah 6:1-8).

100. Lord, in the Name of Jesus pass judgment on any horns that have arisen against me; let Your judgment be appeased and at let rest follow, in the Name of Jesus.

101. Lord, as You are at rest after defeating all enemies, let me too be at rest. Lord, declare a season of rest for me as the season of war is over and I walk in complete victory, in the Name of Jesus.

102. Lord, let me declare: There **GO** the horns, in the Name of Jesus. Never to return – Amen.

103. Lord, let me find and enjoy Your favor and that You will be glorified, in the Name of Jesus.

Warfare Section

104. O, carpenters of God, break the horns of darkness into irreparable pieces, in the Name of Jesus.

105. Now, release tongues of Fire after each of these prayer points.

106. Every power scattering my efforts, I condemn you and shut you down, in the Name of Jesus.

Release tongues of Fire.

107. Every evil arrow fired against my breakthroughs, break now, in the Name of Jesus.

Release tongues of Fire.

108. Lord, arise and defeat the evil archers aiming and firing at me, in the Name of Jesus.

Release tongues of fire.

109. Every power causing stagnation in my life, be disgraced forever, in the Name of Jesus.

Release tongues of Fire.

110. Today, right now, I will lift up my head.
111. Tomorrow, I will lift up my head.
112. Lord, You are the lifter of my head.
113. This week I will lift up my head.
114. This month, this year, I will again lift up my head.
115. Discouragement, GO! In the Name of Jesus.
116. Any spirit or power that has come or been sent to trample down good things in my life, by the power of the Spirit of God, I trample you down instead, in the Name of Jesus.

Release tongues of Fire.

117. Any hunter looking for my destiny, be blinded in the Name of Jesus.

Release tongues of Fire.

118. I break loose, I break free from witchcraft, covens, and altars, in the Name of Jesus.

Release tongues of Fire.

119. All witchcraft thrones in my area that are working against me, be terminated and perish with all your summoning, in the mighty Name of Jesus Christ.

Release tongues of Fire.

120. Blood of Jesus, arise and shatter to desolation all networking and trafficking of witchcraft working against me in the heavens, firmament, air, land, and waters, in the Name of Jesus.

Release tongues of Fire.

121. I command that both the defensive and offensive weapons of my enemies fail to work against me, ever again, in the Name of Jesus, by the power that is in the Blood of Jesus. Amen.

122. Blood of Jesus, break asunder, rebuke and make desolate every program in the heavens that is operating or planning to operate against me through the moon, sun, stars, constellations and any element, in the Name of Jesus.

Release tongues of Fire.

123. By the Fire in the Blood of Jesus, I command all spirits of lust, perversion, adultery, fornication, uncleanness, and immorality to come out of me, my body, my mind, my soul, my spirit, my life, in the Name of Jesus.

Release tongues of Fire.

124. Through the power in the Blood of Jesus, I command all spirits of witchcraft, sorcery, divination, and the occult to come out of my life, in the Name of Jesus.

Release tongues of Fire.

125. Through the Blood of Jesus, I destroy all ancestral *spirits* of freemasonry, idolatry, witchcraft, false religion, polygamy, lust, and perversion, in the Name of Jesus.

Release tongues of Fire.

126. I prevail over curses. (repeat until the Holy Spirit gives you release to stop)

Release tongues of Fire.

Whatever is born of God overcomes the world and this is the victory that has overcome the world, even our faith.

127.   I am born of God.

128.   Saved by grace. I am redeemed by the Blood of the Lamb. I overcome by the Word of my testimony; I prevail over curses.

129.   I overcome generational bondages, in the Name of Jesus.

130.   I prevail over witches, warlocks, wizards, and every evil human agent.

131.   I prevail over evil.

132.   Love is the greatest power; I have Love, I am in Love, Christ is Love; I am in Christ; therefore, I prevail. Therefore, I win.

133.   Therefore, I am the victor, and I have the victory, in the Name of Jesus.

134.   I seal this message, these decrees and declarations and prayers across every realm, age, era, dimension, and timeline, past present and future and to infinity. I seal them with the Blood of Jesus and the Holy Spirit of Promise.

135.   Let every retaliation against this word, these prayers, these decrees and declarations spoken, prayed, or said by the speaker, or heard by the listener, or anyone praying these words backfire without

Mercy, to infinity against the evil perpetrator, in the Name of Jesus. Amen.

Dear Reader

Thank you for acquiring and reading this book. This information really blessed me and I pray it will bless you as well. It is important to know what you are dealing with so you will know how to fight and win! Remember, in Christ, we always win.

God bless you,

Dr. Marlene Miles

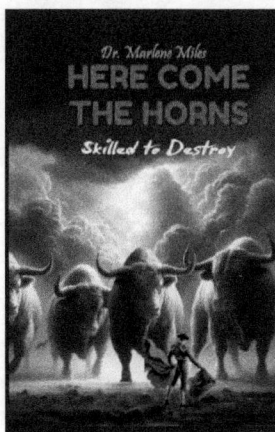

Appendix

A carpenter is an artificer a graver, as seen in Exodus 25:25, Hosea 28:11 and 1 Chronicles 13:2. Nehemiah 11:35, 2 Samuel 5:11.

A carpenter is a worker in metals as seen in 1 Samuel 13:19, Hosea 8:6, and 13:2; Deuteronomy 27:15, Jeremiah 10:9, Isaiah 40:19, 41:7, 54:16, 1 Chronicles 29:5, 2 Chronicles 24:12.

A carpenter could work in wood, as in 2 Samuel 5:11, 1 Chronicles 14:1, 2 Kings 12:12, 22:6, 2 Chronicles 34:11, Jeremiah 10:3, Isaiah 40:20, 44:13. And in the New Testament, Matthew 13:55 and Mark 6:3.

He could work with stone, 2 Samual 5:11, 1 Chronicles 14:1, Exodus 28:1; Isaiah 45:16, 44:12, Jeremiah 24:1, 29:2,

Prayerbooks by this author

While most books by this author have prayer points either throughout the book or at the end, there are some books that are only prayers. You just open up the book and pray. They are listed below:

Prayers Against Barrenness: *For Success in Business and Life*

Fruit of the Womb: *Prayers Against Barrenness*

Beauty Curses, *Warfare Prayers Against*
https://a.co/d/5Xlc20M

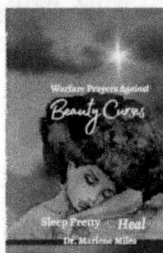

Courts of Marriage: Prayers for Marriage in the Courts of Heaven *(prayerbook)*
https://a.co/d/cNAdgAq

Courtroom Warfare @ Midnight
(prayerbook) https://a.co/d/5fc7Qdp

Demonic Cobwebs *(prayerbook)*
https://a.co/d/fp9Oa2H

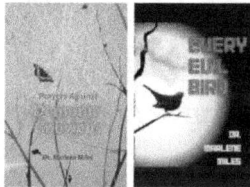

Every Evil Bird https://a.co/d/hF1kh1O

Gates of Thanksgiving

Spirits of Death, Hell & the Grave, Pass Over Me and My House

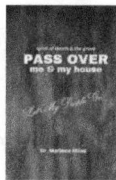

Throne of Grace: Courtroom Prayer

Warfare Prayer Against Poverty
https://a.co/d/bZ61lYu

Other books by this author

AK: The Adventures of the Agape Kid

Already Married in the Spirit: *Why You May Not Be Married in the Natural*

AMONG SOME THIEVES

Ancestral Powers

Anti-Marriage, *The Spirit of*

Backstabbers https://a.co/d/gi8iBxf

Barrenness, *Prayers Against* https://a.co/d/feUltIs

Battlefield of Marriage, *The*

Beware of the Dog: Prayers Against Dogs in the Dream.

Bless Your Food: *Let the Dining Table be Undefiled*

Blindsided: *Has the Old Man Bewitched You?* https://a.co/d/5O2fLLR

Break Free from Collective Captivity

Broken Spirits & Dry Bones

Casting Down Imaginations

Churchzilla, The Wanna-Be, Supposed-to-be Bride of Christ

Demonic Cobwebs (prayerbook)

Demonic Time Bombs

Demons Hate Questions

Devil Loves Trauma, *The*

Devil Weapons: Unforgiveness, Bitterness,…

The Devourers: Thieves of Darkness 2

Do Not Swear by the Moon

Don't Refuse Me, Lord (4 book series)
https://a.co/d/idP34LG

Dream Defilement

The Emptiers: *Thieves of Darkness, 1*
https://a.co/d/5I4n5mc

Evil Touch

Failed Assignment

Fantasy Spirit Spouse
https://a.co/d/hW7oYbX

FAT Demons (The): *Breaking Demonic Curses* https://a.co/d/4kP8wV1

The Fold (5-book series)

- The Fold (Book 1)
- Name Your Seed (Book 2)
- The Poor Attitudes of Money (3)
- Do Not Orphan Your Seed (4)
- For the Sake of the Gospel (5)
- My Sowing Journal

Gang Ups: Touch Not God's Anointed

Getting Rid of Evil Spiritual Food

https://a.co/d/i2L3WYQ

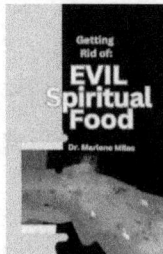

got HEALING? Verses for Life

got LOVE? Verses for Life

got HOPE? Verses for Life

got money? https://a.co/d/g2av41N

Here Come the Horns: *Skilled to Destroy*
https://a.co/d/cZiNnkP

How to Dental Assist

How to Dental Assist2: Be Productive, Not Wasteful

How to STOP Being a Blind Witch or Warlock

I Take It Back

Legacy

Let Me Have A Dollar's Worth
https://a.co/d/h8F8XgE

Level the Playing Field

Living for the NOW of God

Lose My Location
https://a.co/d/crD6mV9

Love Breaks Your Heart

Made Perfect In Love

Man Safari, *The*

Marriage Ed. Rules of Engagement & Marriage

Made Perfect in Love

Money Hunters: Beware of Those

Money on the Altar https://a.co/d/4EqJ2Nr

Mulberry Tree, *The* https://a.co/d/9nR9rRb

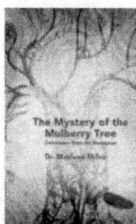

Motherboard (The) - *Soul Prosperity Series*

Name Your Seed

Occupy: *Until I Return*

Plantation Souls

Players Gonna Play

Power Money: Nine Times the Tithe

https://a.co/d/gRt41gy

The Power of Wealth *(forthcoming)*

Powers Above

The Robe, Part 1, The Lessons of Joseph

The Robe, Part II, The Lessons of Joseph

Seasons of Grief

Seasons of Waiting

Seasons of War

Second Marriage, Third--, *Any Marriage*

https://a.co/d/6m6GN4N

Sift You Like Wheat

Six Men Short: What Has Happened to all the Men?

Soul Prosperity soul prosperity series 3

https://a.co/d/5p8YvCN

Souls Captivity soul prosperity series 2

The Spirit of Anti-Marriage

The Spirit of Poverty

StarStruck

SUNBLOCK

The Swallowers: *Thieves of Darkness*, 3

Take It Back

This Is NOT That: How to Keep Demons from Coming at You

Time Is of the Essence

Too Many Wives: *Why You Have Lady Problems*

Tormenting Spirits
https://a.co/d/dAogEJf

Toxic Souls

Triangular Power *(series)*

- Powers Above
- SUNBLOCK
- Do Not Swear by the Moon
- STARSTRUCK

Unbreak My Heart: *Don't Let Me Die*

Uncontested Doom

Unguarded Hours, *The*

Unseen Life, *The* (forthcoming)

Upgrade: How to Get Out of Survival Mode

- Toxic Souls (Book 2 of series)
- Legacy (Book 3 of series)

The Wasters: *Thieves of Darkness*, Bk 2
https://a.co/d/bUvI9Jo

What Have You to Declare? What Do You Have With You from Where You've Been?

When I Was A Child, *I Prayed As a Child*

When the Devourer is Rebuked

https://a.co/d/1HVv8oq

The Wilderness Romance *(series)* This series is about conducting a Godly relationship and marriage with someone who is a Wilderness person. It is about how to recognize it and navigate through it. These books are about how not to get caught up in such.

- *The Social Wilderness*
- *The Sexual Wilderness*
- *The Spiritual Wilderness*

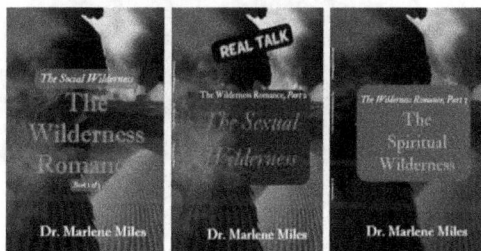

Other Series

The Fold (a series on Godly finances)
https://a.co/d/4hz3unj

Soul Prosperity Series https://a.co/d/bz2M42q

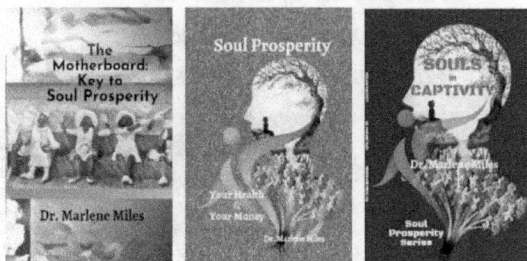

Spirit Spouse books

https://a.co/d/9VehDSo

https://a.co/d/97sKOwm

Battlefield of Marriage, The

https://a.co/d/eUDzizO

Players Gonna Play

https://a.co/d/2hzGw3N

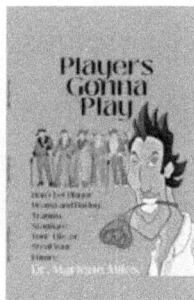

Matters of the Heart

Made Perfect in Love
https://a.co/d/70MQW3O

Love Breaks Your Heart
https://a.co/d/4KvuQLZ

Unbreak My Heart https://a.co/d/84ceZ6M

Broken Spirits & Dry Bones
https://a.co/d/e6iedNP

Thieves of Darkness series

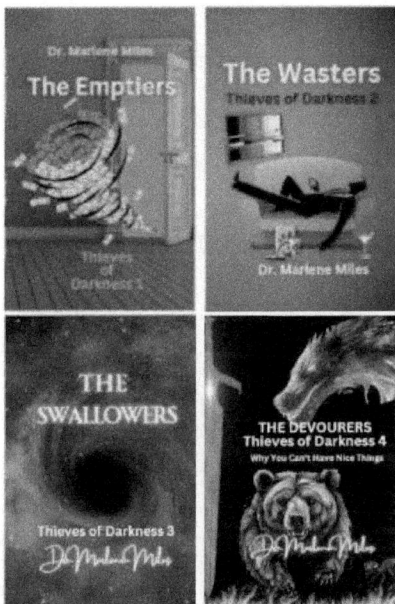

The Emptiers https://a.co/d/heio0dO

The Wasters https://a.co/d/5TG1iNQ

The Swallowers https://a.co/d/1jWhM6G

The Devourers: Why We Can't Have Nice Things
https://a.co/d/87Tejbf

Triangular Powers https://a.co/d/aUCjAWC

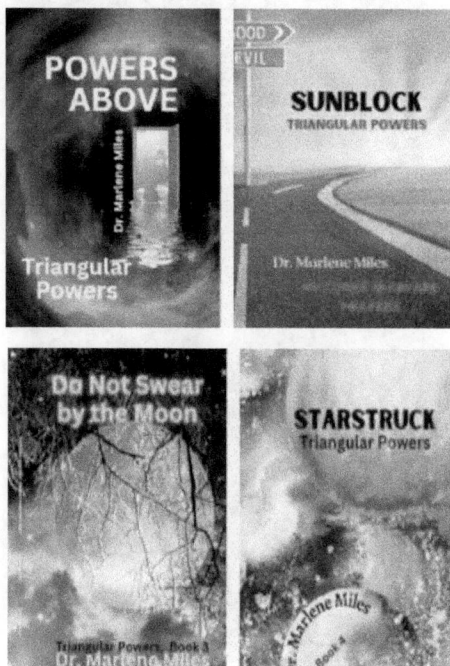

Upgrade (series) *How to Get Out of Survival Mode* https://a.co/d/aTERhXO